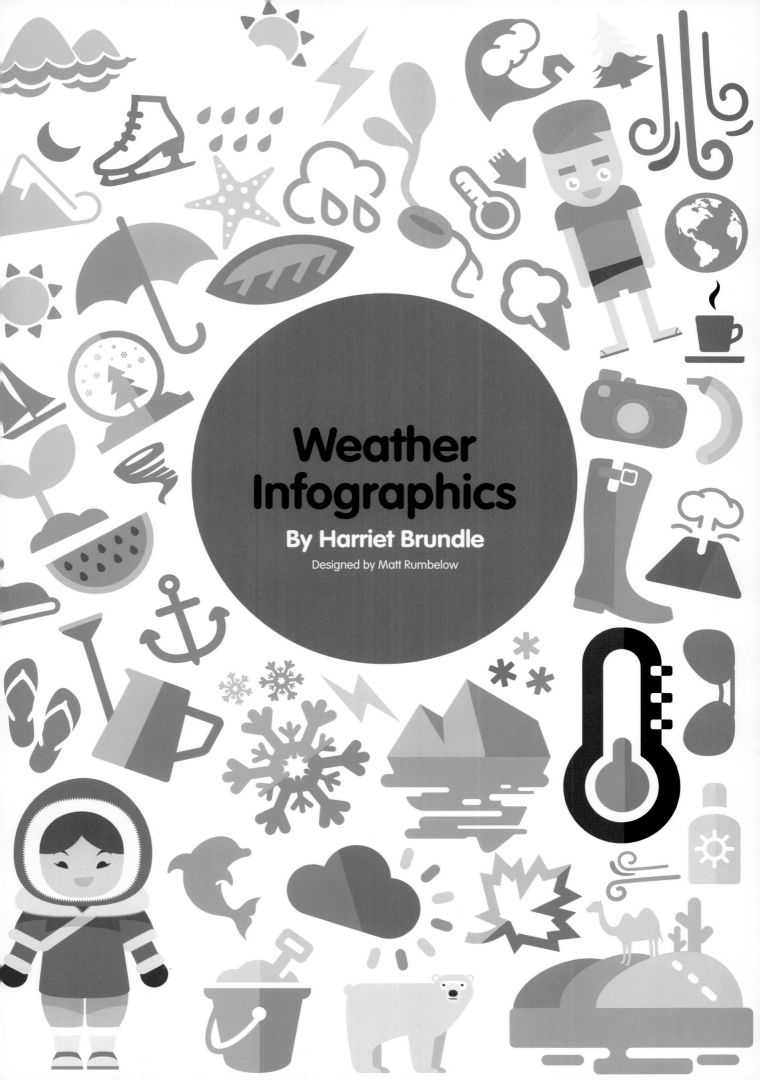

Weather
Infographics

By Harriet Brundle

Designed by Matt Rumbelow

©2017
Book Life
King's Lynn
Norfolk PE30 4LS

ISBN: 978-1-78637-083-9

Written by:
Harriet Brundle

Edited by:
Grace Jones

Designed by:
Matt Rumbelow

A catalogue record
for this book is
available from
the British Library.

BookLife
Publishing
.com

Weather
Infographics

Contents

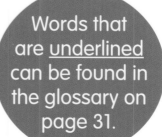

Words that are underlined can be found in the glossary on page 31.

Weather

Weather is all around us. Although we cannot control it, it is an important part of our lives. Weather can take many different forms and it can sometimes express many of these forms at the same time.

Weather is different all over the world. This map shows some of the most extreme weather ever to be recorded.

Death Valley in California, America, has been recorded as the hottest place on Earth. The temperature was recorded at:

56.7°C.

Vostok Station, a Soviet owned research facility in Antarctica, recorded the coldest temperature ever on Earth. In 1983, the temperature reached a record low of:

-89.2°C.

Mawsynram in India receives an average rainfall of 11,871mm of rain every year, making it the wettest place on Earth.

11,871

The types of food that we can grow also depends on the weather.

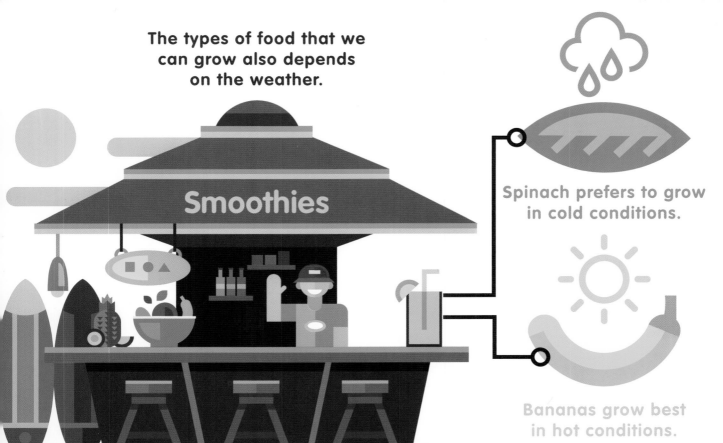

Spinach prefers to grow in cold conditions.

Bananas grow best in hot conditions.

Climate

The climate of an area is the most common type of weather that an area has over a long period of time. Climate is the average pattern of weather, rather than the day-to-day conditions.

spring

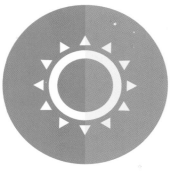

summer

autumn

winter

49°c

The climate in the desert, for example the Sahara, is very hot and has very little rainfall.

-49°c

The climate around the South Pole is extremely cold. The average temperature in winter is -49°c.

Climate change refers to a long-term shift in weather patterns. In recent years, scientific research has shown that the average temperature on Earth is increasing. This is called global warming. It has begun to cause large-scale changes around the world.

Glaciers made out of ice are melting.

Warm seasons are starting earlier and lasting longer.

Sea levels are rising.

Climate change also affects animals all over the world. Habitats are being reduced in size and migration patterns are changing.

A person who studies climates is called a climatologist.

Temperature

Temperature is the measurement of heat in an object or environment. Temperature can be measured using a thermometer.

Liquid water freezes and turns into ice at 0°C.

Liquid water boils and turns into steam at 100°C.

We use temperature as one way to show the weather conditions in a particular place.

The temperature in Egypt in the month of July is an average of 37.5°C.

The temperature in Iceland in July is an average of 13°C.

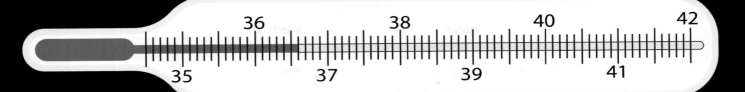

1714

The mercury-in-glass thermometer was invented in 1714. It is made out of very thin glass that has a small amount of metallic liquid called mercury inside it. When the temperature increases, the mercury <u>expands</u> and rises up the glass tube, telling us the temperature. The opposite happens as the temperature decreases.

4,000,000,000,000

One of the hottest man-made temperatures ever recorded was 4,000,000,000,000°C. That's 250,000 times hotter than the Sun.

**90°C
194°F
363°K**

Temperature is measured in degrees. There are three different temperature scales: Fahrenheit, Celsius and Kelvin.

Absolute zero is the coldest temperature that any substance can reach. It is equal to -273.15°C.

Sunshine

The Sun is the star at the centre of the solar system.

Planet Earth is moving all the time. As it <u>rotates</u>, only some of the Earth faces towards the Sun at any one time. This is why we have day and night.

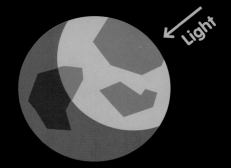

Light

Some countries are hotter than others. Countries that are closer to the <u>equator</u> are often hotter because the Sun remains almost directly overhead all day.

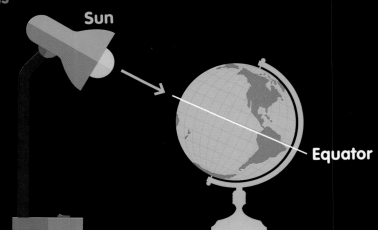

Sun

Equator

The city of Yuma, in Arizona, receives an average of 11 hours of sunlight a day. This makes it one of the sunniest places on Earth!

ARIZONA

8

After it has left the Sun, it takes about 8 minutes for sunlight to reach Earth.

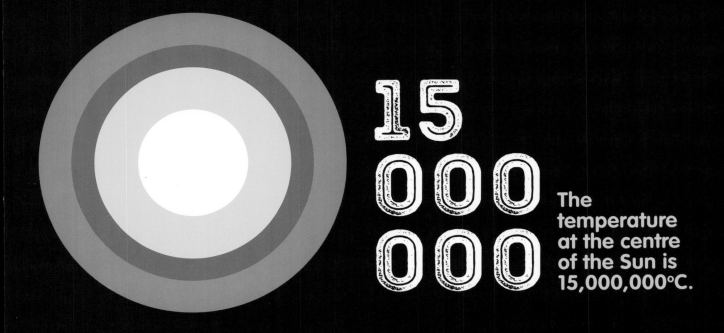

15 000 000

The temperature at the centre of the Sun is 15,000,000°C.

Clouds and Wind

When warm air rises, it cools. As it cools, tiny droplets of moisture are formed. This process is called condensation. When billions of droplets come together, a cloud is made.

Some types of cloud include:

Cirrus

Altostratus

Cumulus

Fog is a type of cloud that appears very close to the ground.

Wind is air that is moving around Earth. It can be a soft breeze or an extremely powerful gust.

What causes wind?

1. The Sun heats the Earth's surface.

2. Some parts of the Earth receive more heat than others and so the air in some places is warmer than in others.

3. As the warm air rises upwards, cooler air rushes in to replace it; this causes wind.

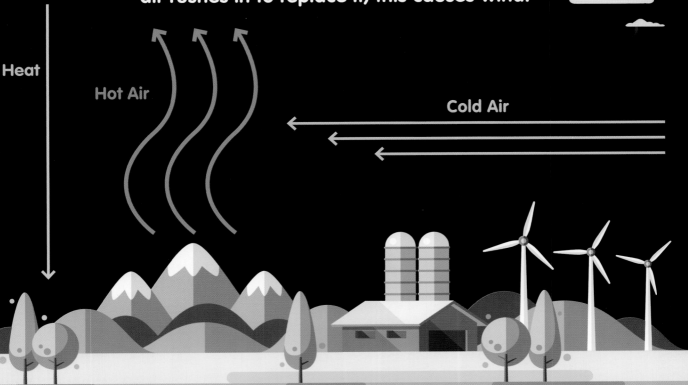

Heat

Hot Air

Cold Air

The Beaufort scale is often used to measure wind intensity. It is done by observing sea conditions.

Rain And Floods

As lots of droplets gather together to form clouds, they become heavy and gravity eventually causes the moisture to fall as rain. Rain is a type of <u>precipitation</u>.

Rain occurs in two main forms:

Shower: heavy, fast rain that lasts for a short period of time

Drizzle: slow, light rain that can last for hours

Rain also might contain dust, dirt, grass and small insects.

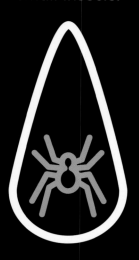

Rain with high acid content is called acid rain. It can be extremely harmful to plants and animals.

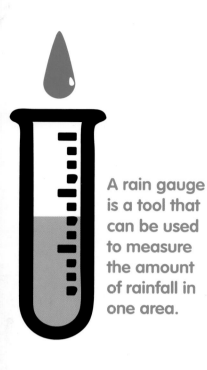

A rain gauge is a tool that can be used to measure the amount of rainfall in one area.

A flood is an overflow of water on to land that would normally be dry.

Floods can occur because of heavy rain or melting snow. River water levels rise and go over their banks.

Flash flooding occurs very quickly, usually within a few hours of heavy rain. The water flows rapidly and can be extremely dangerous.

1 Bn
Every minute, around one billion tons of rain falls onto Earth's surface.

Snow

Snow is formed when water droplets in the clouds turn to ice. For this to happen, the temperature must be below 0°C.

Each droplet becomes an ice crystal. The ice crystals begin to join together to make the start of a snowflake. When the snowflake is heavy enough, it falls to the ground.

No two snowflakes look the same.

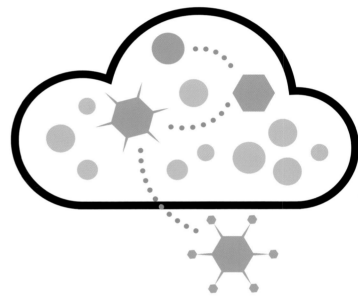

Each winter in the U.S.A., 1,000,000,000,000,000, 000,000,000 ice crystals fall from the sky!

6.3 FEET

Silver Lake in Colorado, U.S.A. received 6.3 feet of snow in a single day in 1921.

Snow will return to its liquid state if the temperature rises above 0°C.

-2°C

3°C

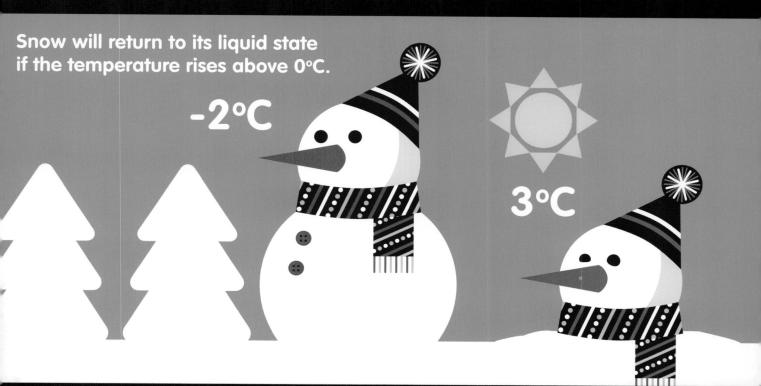

Heavy snowfalls are called snowstorms. If there is a snowstorm with high winds, it is called a blizzard.

Thunder and Lightning

Thunderstorms are storms where you can see lightning and hear thunder. They develop when the <u>atmosphere</u> is very unstable.

As small droplets of ice in the clouds hit into each other, it creates an electrical charge. This produces the flash of light that we can see, called lightning.

When a bolt of lightning breaks through the clouds, it causes the air around it to expand.

As the air <u>contracts</u> back into its normal state, it causes particles in the air to vibrate, which we hear as thunder.

We see lightning before we hear thunder because light travels faster than sound.

Light: **299,792,458** metres per second

Sound: **340** metres per second

÷ 5 = ?

Count the number of seconds between when you see the lightning and when you hear the thunder, divide this number by 5 and this = the number of miles away the thunderstorm is from you.

The sound of thunder moves at around 767 mph. That's eleven times faster than a cheetah!

The average temperature of lightning is estimated to be 20,000°C. That's about as hot as 100 ovens combined.

The Water Cycle

The water cycle is the process by which water continuously moves around the world, from the land to the sky and back again. The Earth has a limited amount of water and the same water keeps going around the water cycle.

2. Condensation

The vapour cools and changes back into a liquid. As a result, clouds are formed.

3. Precipitation

As the water droplets get bigger and heavier, they fall to the ground as rain or snow.

4. Collection

As the precipitation reaches the Earth's surface, some water droplets will fall on land and others will fall back into lakes, rivers and oceans.

1. Evaporation

Water in lakes, rivers and oceans is heated by the sun. The heat causes the water to turn into water vapour that rises up into the air.

The amount of water on Earth is limited, so it is important that we are careful with how we use the water we have. To help save water, we can:

Turn off the tap while brushing our teeth.

Use the shower for less time.

use a watering can and not a hosepipe to water plants in the garden.

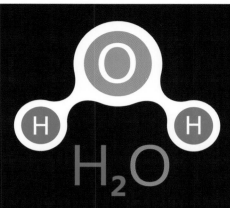

H_2O

Water is sometimes referred to as H20. This is because water is made of two parts Hydrogen and one part Oxygen.

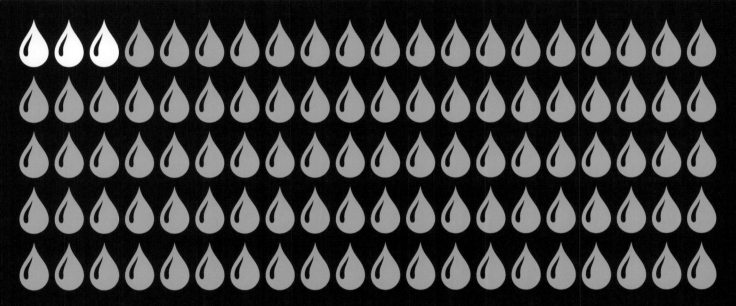

Only around **3% of the water** on Earth is fresh water that we can drink.

A dripping tap wastes at least 5,500 litres of water a year.

The water from your tap could contain the same water molecules that dinosaurs drank!

Animals

All animals adapt over time, meaning that they are often well suited to the weather conditions in their habitat.

Climate change impacts animals in lots of different ways:

Loss of habitat

Warmer temperatures change breeding and <u>hibernation</u> patterns

Rising sea levels can cause flooding and the <u>contamination</u> of habitats

Meerkats have dark circles around their eyes that act like sunglasses, helping them to see when the sun is shining!

Kangaroos use their spit to help themselves to cool off during hot Australian summers. They lick their legs, which helps them to maintain a stable body temperature.

This camel lives in the hot, sandy desert, where it hardly ever rains.

Camels sometimes have to go for months without food in the desert, so they have big humps where they can store fat that can be used for energy.

Thick, bushy eye brows help to shade the camel's eyes from the Sun.

The camel has thick lips so that it can eat prickly desert plants without any pain.

The camel has wide feet so that it can walk more easily on hot sand.

The tarantula spider can survive for more than two years without food.

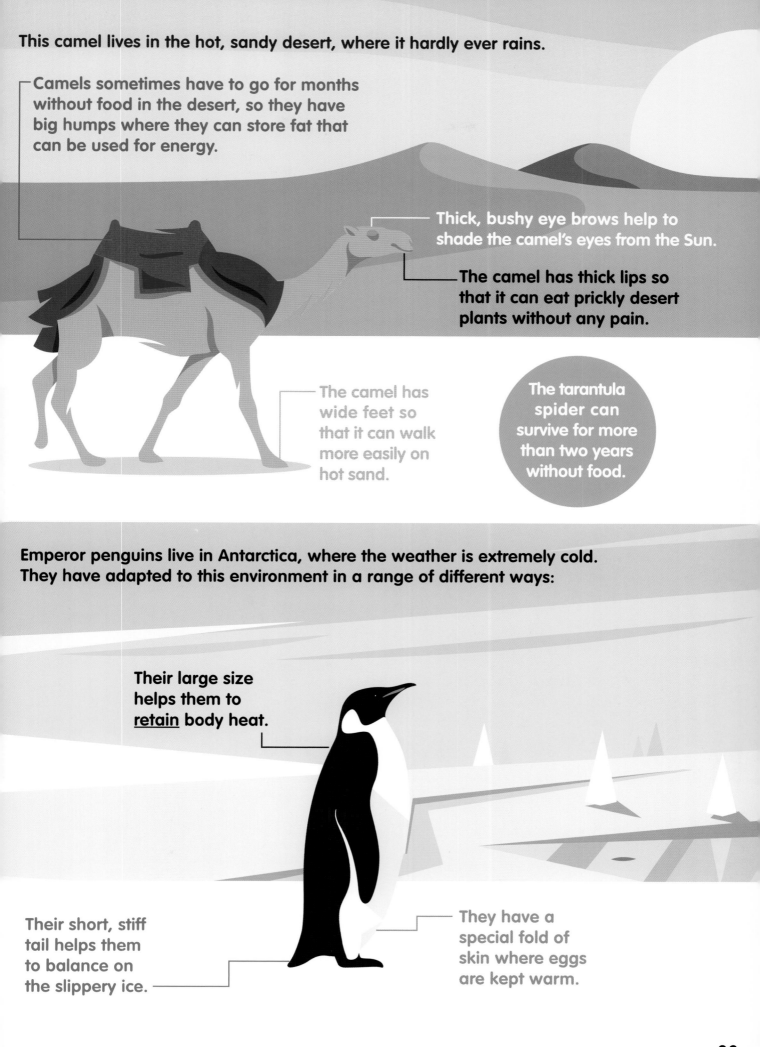

Emperor penguins live in Antarctica, where the weather is extremely cold. They have adapted to this environment in a range of different ways:

Their large size helps them to <u>retain</u> body heat.

Their short, stiff tail helps them to balance on the slippery ice.

They have a special fold of skin where eggs are kept warm.

The Seasons

There are four seasons:
spring, summer, autumn and winter.

Spring

Temperatures begin to get warmer but there is some wind and rain. Baby animals are born and plants begin to blossom.

Summer

This is the warmest season and there is often very little wind or rain. There are more hours of daylight in a day than in any other season.

Autumn

The temperature starts to cool. The hours of daylight become less each day. The trees shed their leaves and animals begin to grow

Winter

This is the coldest season. Temperatures become very cold and in many places there is often rain, sleet, hail or snow.

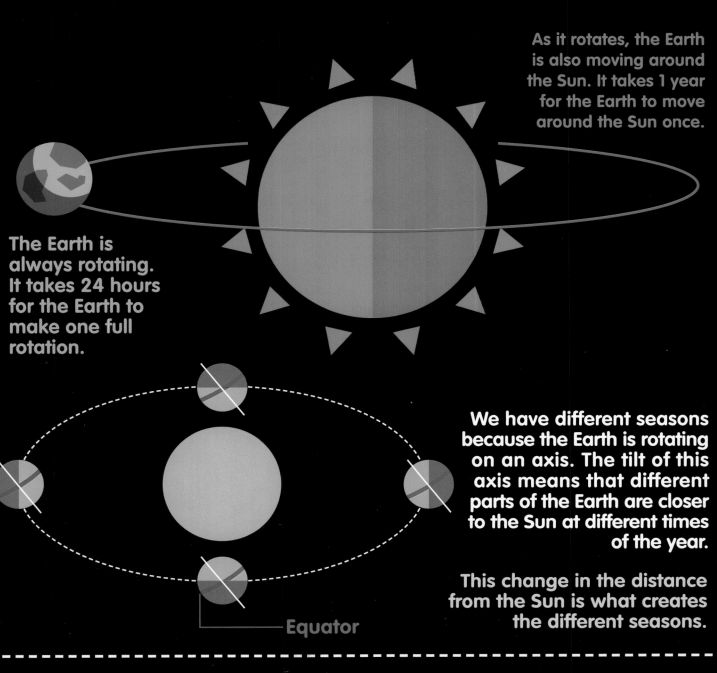

As it rotates, the Earth is also moving around the Sun. It takes 1 year for the Earth to move around the Sun once.

The Earth is always rotating. It takes 24 hours for the Earth to make one full rotation.

We have different seasons because the Earth is rotating on an axis. The tilt of this axis means that different parts of the Earth are closer to the Sun at different times of the year.

This change in the distance from the Sun is what creates the different seasons.

Equator

In England, Christmas time is often extremely cold and there may even be snow. In Australia, Christmas is often celebrated with a BBQ in the sunshine.

Extreme Weather

Hurricanes are large, swirling storms that cause heavy rain and strong winds. They begin over open ocean, but if they reach land they can cause damage to buildings and cars.

Hurricane wind speeds are normally at least 74 mph.

A tornado is a column of air that violently rotates. It is in contact with both the land and the clouds.

The eye of a hurricane can be over 200 miles in diameter.

Tornadoes are particularly dangerous. The most intense tornadoes can completely destroy large buildings and throw cars over 100 metres from where they started.

300

The wind speed of a tornado can reach 300 mph.

1,000

On average, there are around 1,000 tornadoes reported each year.

**20cm
1kg**

The largest hail stone to ever fall was recorded in South Dakota in 2010.

The average thunderstorm is between 6 and 10 miles wide.

Hundreds of thunderstorms are happening all around the world right now!

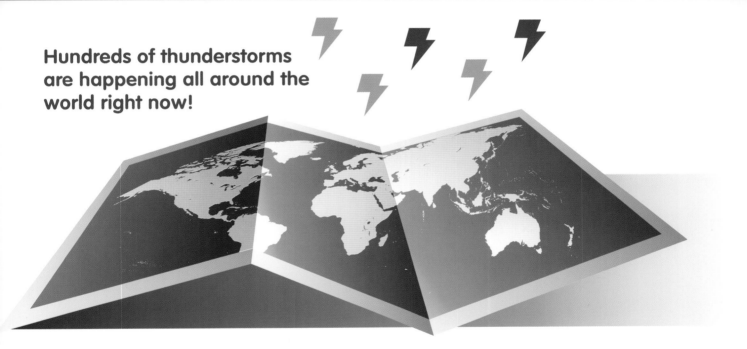

Droughts are long periods of time with little or no rain. When a major drought occurs, crops fail and food supplies run low, which can have devastating effects on those living in the area.

Weather Forecasting

Weather forecasting is the process of **predicting** what the weather might be like in the future.

This is what a weather forecast over a week might look like:

LONDON, UK   MONDAY 21

Partly Cloudy

25°/ 17°   37 %   3 m/s SW

| TUE 22 | WED 23 | THU 24 |
| FRI 25 | SAT 26 | SUN 27 |

Weather forecasters put their predictions onto a map so that we can see what the weather will be like where we live.

Forecasters use a combination of computer data, information received from satellites in the sky, weather observations and weather patterns to predict what the weather will be.

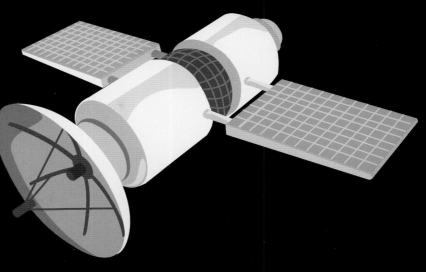

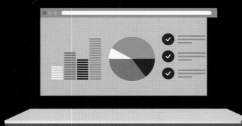

Weather forecasters measure lots of different factors, including temperature, wind speed and precipitation.

Forecasters can also predict levels of humidity, which are the different percentages of water vapour in the air.

Our bodies sweat if we are too hot as the moisture is intended to cool us down. However, if the air is extremely humid already, our sweat does not evaporate from our skin and so we feel like the temperature is much hotter than it really is.

Bellingham in Washington, U.S.A. has an extremely high humidity level of 79.4%.

Activity

Make your own rain gauge!

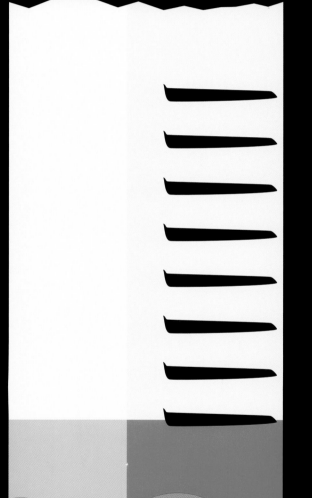

Make sure that you have an adult to help you.

Step 1. Using scissors, carefully remove the top of a large plastic bottle so that you have an even sized container to catch the rainfall in.

Step 2. Fill the bottom part of the bottle with small stones or pebbles that will not absorb any of the rain water. This will provide weight so that the gauge will stay upright even if the weather is windy.

Step 3. On the side of the bottle, use a ruler and a marker pen to mark each centimetre from the bottom to the top.

Step 4. Fill the container up to the nearest cm so that all the pebbles are covered. This is to make sure you have a level starting point.

Step 5. Place the gauge outside on level ground and make sure it has nothing above it, for example the branches of trees.

Step 6. Check your rain gauge every 24 hours to find out how much rain has fallen. You can see how much water has fallen by checking the waterline straight on at eye level. Once you have a measurement, record it, empty the gauge of water (but keep the same pebbles every time) and refill to start again.

Top Tip! Try doing this at different times of the year so that you can monitor how the seasons affect the amount of rainfall.

Glossary

adapt   change to suit different conditions

atmosphere   the mixture of gases that make up the air and surround the Earth

contamination   to make something poisonous or less pure

contracts   becomes smaller

equator   the imaginary line around the Earth that is an equal distance from the North and South Poles

expands   becomes bigger

glaciers   large masses of ice that move slowly

habitats   the natural environments in which animals or plants live

hibernation   when an animal spends the winter sleeping

migration   movement from one place to another

precipitation   water that falls from the clouds

predicting   to say that an event will happen in the future

retain   to keep or maintain something

rotates   to turn around a central point or axis

Index